All the way from **A** to

The **ABC's** of Health

Written by Peter Alderman
Illustrated by Mark Kummer

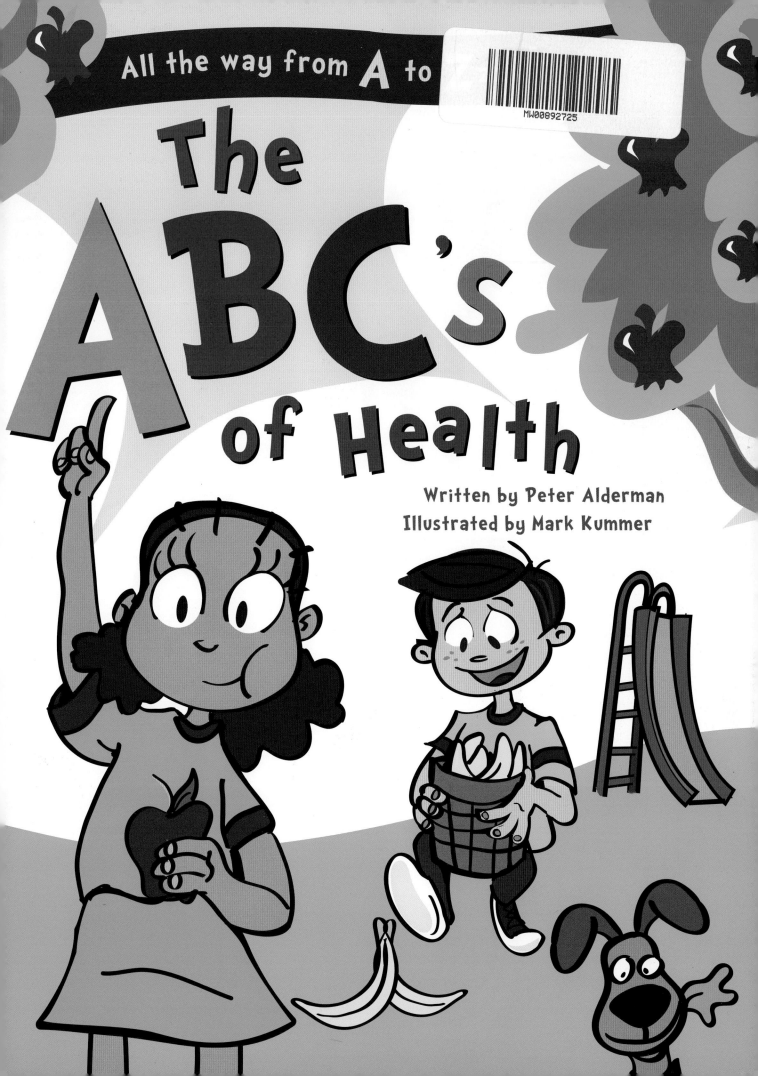

A is for Apples.
They're good for the heart.
They're tasty and sweet.
Now, that's a good start.

B is for Bananas.
They help muscles rest.
When muscles relax,
that's when they work best.

Bananas give you a potassium punch, which keeps your muscles from cramping.

E is for Eggs.
They taste really great,
so scrambled or poached,
put lots on your plate!

F is for Fruits,
nature's sweet treat.
They make you feel well
from your ears to your feet.

Fruits' vitamins and
minerals give you energy,
while their fiber makes your
tummy happy!

G is for Grapes,
grown on vines that climb.
Eat them like Romans—
a bunch at a time!

H is for Healthy.
Let's eat the right way,
so we feel our best
when we go to play.

Healthful foods provide energy to jump higher and run faster than you ever thought you could!

I is for Iron,
which helps fight diseases.
A good thing to know
when your best friend sneezes!

J is for Juice,
which helps when you're sick.
A big glass of OJ
might help do the trick.

A glass of orange juice has 120 milligrams of vitamin C—all you need to kick that icky cold!

K

K is for Kale,
a green, leafy treat.
It's a superfood,
so have more to eat!

L is for Lemons.
They're packed with power.
Don't eat them too fast—
lemons are sour.

Kale is full of antioxidants! It might just be the biggest food superhero out there!

O is for Oranges.
They're juicy inside.
You can't rhyme with orange.
Trust me—I've tried.

P is for Peas.
They're fun and they're round.
They help you to grow.
Eat them by the pound.

These little green spheres are wonderful sources of almost 20 vitamins and minerals!

Q is for Quiet
that helps you to rest,
which everyone needs,
so we do our best.

R is for Raisins—
grapes left in the sun.
They're much smaller now.
Eating them is fun.

U is for Us.
We've learned a whole bunch
about good healthy foods
we should pack in our lunch.

V is for Vitamins
in every good meal.
The more that you get,
the better you feel.

Eating a colorful rainbow of foods gives your body the vitamins it needs to be as healthy as it can be!

W is for Water,
refreshing and nice.
Drink water all day,
but don't crunch the ice!

X is for eXercise.
We need some each day.
So, hop off the couch,
go outside, and play!

Walking, running,
jumping, riding bikes, and
playing tag are all awesome
ways to exercise.

Let's Review!

A

Apples help your lungs grow strong and healthy, and protect them from asthma, too!

B

Bananas give you a potassium punch, which keeps your muscles from cramping.

C

Carrots help your eyes to work their best—especially at night when it's dark!

D

Calcium in dairy makes your bones strong, and probiotics in yogurt fight diseases.

E

Eggs are a perfect protein: they give your body every ingredient it needs to build muscle!

F

Fruits' vitamins and minerals give you energy, while their fiber makes your tummy happy!

G

Grapes are packed with vitamin K—a vitamin almost everyone needs more of to help fight infection.

H

Healthful foods provide energy to jump higher and run faster than you ever thought you could!

I

Everyone needs iron, found in red meat, nuts, and spinach, to have strength and energy!

J

A glass of orange juice has 120 milligrams of vitamin C—all you need to kick that icky cold!

K

Kale is full of antioxidants! It might just be the biggest food superhero out there!

L

The vitamin C in lemons kills "free radicals" in your body that try to make you sick.

M

Milk makes your teeth strong and healthy. Drink milk and you'll have the happiest mouth around!

N

Eating nuts keeps your stomach full and gives you the energy to work and play.

O

Oranges are packed with vitamin C, which helps your body stay healthy!

P

These little green spheres are wonderful sources of almost 20 vitamins and minerals!

Q

When you sleep, your body knits back together any parts you injured during the day.

R

Raisins give your body a quick boost of energy through iron, vitamin B, and potassium.

S

There are more nutrients in spinach than in almost any other food. It's a secret weapon!

T

Tomatoes contain the antioxidant "lycopene," which helps your heart beat healthy and strong!

U

Bringing a healthful lunch gives us the energy to do our best in school and play!

V

Eating a colorful rainbow of foods gives your body the vitamins it needs to be as healthy as it can be!

W

Water is very important. If your body isn't getting enough, it'll let you know by making you feel thirsty!

X

Walking, running, jumping, riding bikes, and playing tag are all awesome ways to exercise.

Y

Your body needs to be filled with all different wonderful healthful foods to help you feel your best.

Z

Most kids need about 10 hours of sleep—so, snuggle up tight and sweet dreams!